#prehistoric
FOLLOW THE DINOSAURS

Scholastic Inc.

28
photos

310
followers

90,026
following

Author: JOHN OWEN

Library of Congress Cataloging-in-Publication Data available

ISBN 978-0-545-82341-8

10 9 8 7 6 5 4 3 2 1   15 16 17 18 19

Printed in China 67
First edition, March 2015
Book design by Jessica Meltzer

TABLEOFCONTENTS

TABLEOFCONTENTS

#prehistoric
FOLLOW THE DINOSAURS

1
photos

0
followers

0
following

North America

Username: INTERRUPTINGDINO

Name: Iguanodon (iguana tooth)

Period: Cretaceous (135–125 million years ago)

Size: 30 feet long, 16 feet tall – with 6-inch spikes on my thumbs!

Diet: Plants 4 lyfe 🤢

Hangouts: North America, North Africa, Europe

Bio: WHOOHOO FIRST DINO ON HERE!! I'm about that selfie life. Right now, I'm all by my selfie. #irock #iroll #irule

★ 59 LOVES

 HELLO! WELCOME! I have an absolutely ENORMOUS announcement! That's right . . . I am #THRILLED to announce . . . THAT I JUST TOOK THIS SELFIE!! #BOOM! #INSTADINO! #SUPERCOOL! #PrehistoryInTheMaking!

 INTERRUPTINGDINO Yello? #partyof1

132 photos

1,000 followers

1.2M following

Ancient Ocean Floors

Username: TRILL_O_BYTE
Name: Trilobite (three-lobed)
Period: Cambrian through the Permian (541–251 million years ago . . . What about you? Oh, you've been around for 8–12 years? Nice! You've only got, what, 270,999,992 years to go?!)
Size: One trilobite. I ran the scene for such a long time that I don't really measure myself by anyone else's standards.
Diet: Delicious, nutritious scum. Yum!
Hangouts: The floors of every ancient ocean.
Bio: I'm one of the most numerous animals in the ancient seas. And, oh, as if that weren't "enough"? Well, ever heard of insects? Oh, you have? I'm an early ancestor to all of them. #ThatsTrill

⭐ **201 LOVES**

Hang time with my clique. Bffs #4lyfe #Byte4eva

 TRILL_O_BYTE2 Best party on the ocean floor! 😛

 TRILL_O_BYTE5 We takin' over!! 😎

 TRILL_O_BYTE VIT* ONLY! *(very important trilobites)!

15
photos

105
followers

372
following

Shallow Seas Near Europe

Username: TERRORGOTYA
Name: Pterygotus (wing-animal)
Period: Silurian (443–419 million years ago)
Size: 7 feet 4 inches
Diet: Anything in the sea. Watch out!
Hangouts: Shallow seas of North America/Europe
Bio: I'm a #SeaScorpion. Wait, you guys don't have those anymore? Are you sure? I mean, I was really scary and successful for my time. I feel like I would have stuck around. Oh! Wait! Maybe I turned invisible so that I could be even more deadly. Yeah, that must be what happened.

★ **44 LOVES**

✒ Claw party! #ancientinsectancestor #fearsomepredator #killerinstinct

 @HORSESHOECRAB Hey, buddy. Saw your "about me" section. Don't worry, man! I'm your descendant.

 TERRORGOTYA PHEW, @HorseshoeCrab. 😃 I knew we couldn't just be GONE. Wow, a crab the size of a horse! My relatives are huge! Let me just click on your link to see how big you guys really are. WAIT . . . WHAT THE?!!?!

21 photos

707 followers

291 following

Morocco

Username: DUNKLE_BONE
Name: Dunkleosteus ("Dunkle's bone." Your guess is as good as mine there. If I ever meet the guy who named me . . . Let's just say I'm going to bite him with my #hugejaws.)
Period: Devonian (374–360 million years ago)
Size: Bigger than a great white shark
Diet: Carnivore (I had a bite MORE powerful than a great white.)
Hangouts: Morocco, Belgium, Poland, North America
Bio: I'm an armor-plated fish and the greatest predator of my time. I was the biggest animal ever before the dinosaurs came along. Gosh, I'd like to bite them. #soreloser

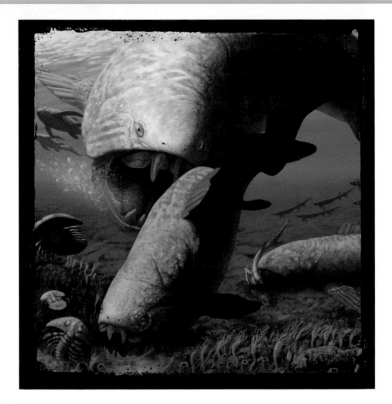

⭐ **122 LOVES**

↩️ Say cheese! #badtothebone #strongbite #SchoolBusSized

 OFFICIAL_REX1 Did somebody say bite?

 DUNKLE_BONE @Official_Rex1 I'm not scared of you! My bite is as strong as yours! 🥴

52
photos

1,054
followers

537
following

Europe

Username: HAIRTIPSFORSHARKS
Name: Stethacanthus (chest spike)
Period: Devonian to Carboniferous (390–360 million years ago)
Size: 6 feet long, 100 pounds
Diet: Smaller sharks and other fish
Hangouts: North America, Europe
Bio: As an ancient shark, it's always important to look good. If we're gonna be around for millions of years, we better always look #pictureready. #GetYourHairRight and the #RestWillFollow. #wordstoliveby

★ 33 LOVES

Bored with your look? Try a bumpy and toothlike updo! #protip #hair101

 HAMMERHEADHILARY Having a great hammer day thanks to you @hairtipsforsharks. 😊

 HAIRTIPSFORSHARKS Thanks for the love, @hammerheadhilary. Keep checking back for our sharktip swag.

172 photos

2,347 followers

129 following

Northern Canada

Username: ADVENTUROUSAMPHIBIAN

Name: Tiktaalik (the word for a type of fish in the Inuit language used in the territory I was discovered!)

Period: Devonian (375 million years ago)

Size: 10 feet long

Diet: #Surf? Check. #Turf? Check. #NoPickyEatersHere

Hangouts: Nunavut, Northern Canada

Bio: Follow me as I use my primitive legs, primitive lung-like gills, and extraordinary bravery to go where no amphibians have gone before!

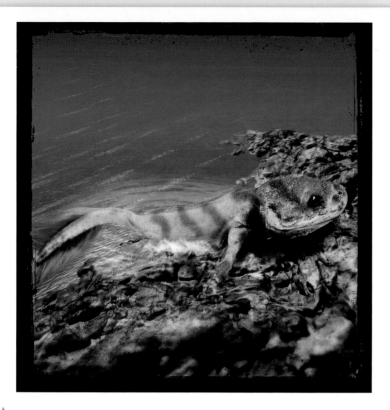

⭐ 1 LOVE

〜 Here we are, folks! I am about to attempt to use my #slightlyleglike fins to #push myself onto the #finalfrontier: land! Follow along in the comments below!

 ADVENTUROUSAMPHIBIAN All right! This is it! There's no turning back now. This is #onesmallstep for me, #onegiantleap for future amphibian kind . . .

 ADVENTUROUSAMPHIBIAN . . . AND I'M HERE! I'm up here, in the air! I'm #FLOPPING all around. I look super #awkward.

 ADVENTUROUSAMPHIBIAN And now, #victorious, I will slip back into the water, as any more time up here would #drymeout.

72
photos

135
followers

202
following

North American Forests

Username: #1_REPTILIA
Name: Hylonomus (forest mouse)
Period: Carboniferous (359–299 million years ago)
Size: 1 foot long, 1 pound
Diet: insects #mmmmm
Hangouts: Forests of North America
Bio: I'm the first modern reptile. That's right – lizards, snakes, and crocodiles all wish they could be me. Life was hard for a little while without any friends, but now that I'm on land, I'm living the good life. #dollabillz #getmoney

⭐ **82 LOVES**

✎ #MovingOnUp. These new #eggs with #shells of mine mean that I can live on land full-time. Now the only time you'll see me by the water's edge is when I'm #catchingsomerays by the pool. #thefinerthings #richreptilesofinstagram

 ADVENTUROUSAMPHIBIAN hey @#1_Reptilia where's my #cashmoney? I found that land. #findersfee

102
photos

200
followers

646
following

Wyoming

Username: SUPADUPAFLY
Name: Meganeura
Period: Carboniferous (359–299 million years ago)
Size: An eagle! (aka I'm absolutely ripped for a bug) #gymtime
Diet: Other smaller and weaker insects
Hangouts: Wyoming
Bio: I'm a griffinfly – the biggest insect of all time. I work hard for that title, though. I watch what I eat, and I get plenty of exercise. Sometimes I fly for hours just working off the protein I had for lunch. Insects are delicious!

42 LOVES

Just KILLED #workoutwednesday. It's official: my wings are #twoandahalffeetlong and now I #ruletheskies.

 #1_REPTILIA Mmm, eyes on the flies. #lunch #lookoutbelow

 SUPADUPAFLY Watch out, @#1_reptilia. You haven't seen how ripped I am.

331
photos

243
followers

176
following

Israel

Username: CAPTAIN_COOLIO

Name: Dimetrodon

Period: Permian (299–252 million years ago)

Size: One 6-foot-3-inch man standing on another 6-foot-3-inch man's shoulders

Diet: Carnivore

Hangouts: Israel, Germany, Switzerland, China

Bio: Awwww, yeah. Here I come! I existed before the dinosaurs and I'm more closely related to mammals! And see that big hump on top of my body? That's called a sail. I guess you could call me the Captain. Captain of cool.

★ **1,006 LOVES**

✎ Land ahoy! #nosailgotojail Get it trending, folks! 😎

DOUBLEDIPPER That's pretty good. But how about #youhavearuffle #onyourback?

CAPTAIN_COOLIO #smh . . . so immature. Stop trolling my account. #coolrules

772 photos

401 followers

393 following

Russia

Username: PROMKING15

Name: Estemmenosuchus

Period: Permian (299–252 million years ago)

Size: 13 feet long, 500 pounds

Diet: Herbivorous

Hangouts: Russia

Bio: My name means "crowned crocodile" —I'm taking that as a great sign for the Permian Prom next week! I'm using this account to take selfies so that I can be sure I look my best! Since we don't have mirrors in the Permian, I've never seen what I look like. I'm almost as excited to see my selfie as I am for prom!

The Permian Prom

299–252 million years ago
Russian Countryside
9–12 p.m.

In the event of rain, snow, or the Permian Extinction, prom will be rescheduled for a later date.

★ 13 LOVES

🖊 Okay . . . #testing #testing . . . let's see how this works. All right, taking a #snap of my face. #selfiealert! Now I'll turn this around and finally see just how smokin' hot I really am. #Three . . . #Two . . . #One . . . and #OHNOOOOOOOOOOOOOOOOOOOOOOOOOOOOOOO OOOOOOOOOOOOOOOOOOOOOOOOOOOOOOOOO OOOOOOOOOOOOOOOOOOOOOOOOOOOOOOOOO OOOOOOOOOOOOOOO 😨

101
photos

494
followers

881
following

Texas

Username: DOUBLEDIPPER
Name: Diplocaulus
Period: Permian (299–252 million years ago)
Size: 3 feet long
Diet: Insects and fish
Hangouts: Morocco, Texas
Bio: Sure, my head is shaped a little differently than yours. The better to boomerang you with, my dear! I'm happy in my own skin. #onein251million #unique

◀ 1 ... **22** ... 115 ▶

⭐ **65 LOVES**

✒ Look what I can do! I'll use my own body as a #boomerang right . . . now!

 DOUBLEDIPPER #Ouch #ThatHurt. I really need to stop doing that just to prove my point. 😟

13
photos

721
followers

6,542
following

Russia

Username: TANKSTERINO
Name: Scutosaurus (shield-reptile)
Period: Permian (299–252 million years ago)
Size: 10 feet long, heavy (like super, super heavy)
Diet: Plants
Hangouts: Russia
Bio: Don't I look like I would be fun to ride all around? Think again! I've got spikes along my skull to keep away hitchhikers #keepwalkin #cantridethistank

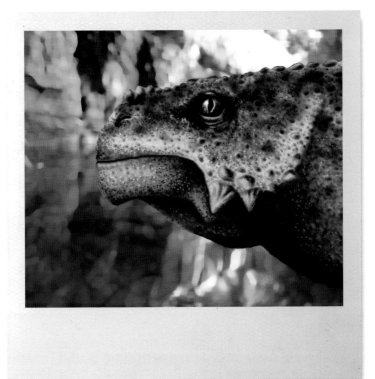

⭐ **30 LOVES**

🖋️ #bigguy. When you're my size, you can't run too fast–but my #thickskin helps protect me from predators. #Takinmytime #everydayarmor

 CAPTAIN_COOLIO we'll see about that . . . see how my #BITES feel!

1 photos

721 followers

1.2M following

Every Place on Earth

Username: XOTHEGREATDYINGXO
Name: The Permian Extinction
Period: 251 million years ago
Size: Hmm. I'm not sure how to describe my size, since I'm not exactly a single thing. I'm really more of an event. So . . . I don't know . . . I guess my size would be "the biggest die-off of all time"? I hope that helps!
Diet: Oh my gosh. I love food! Where to start, really? I love eating about 95 percent of all marine species and 70 percent of all terrestrial species alive in the Permian.
Hangouts: Earth #allmine #badsharer
Bio: Let's see . . . I LOVE volcanoes spewing toxic gas everywhere.

⭐ **100 LOVES**

Don't cry because it's over. 😢 Smile because it's now time for the dinosaurs! 😵

 PROMKING15 thank you. thank you for giving me an excuse to skip prom. #grateful

13
photos

721
followers

6,542
following

Texas

Username: LONESTARLIZARD

Name: Postosuchus

Period: Triassic (252–201 million years ago)

Size: 6.5 feet tall, 20 feet long

Diet: Meat! I'm a Texan after all!!

Hangouts: Texas, baby!

Bio: Go, Texas Longhorns! Shorthorns, too. Any of the #herbivores I like to eat, really. It's so fun to jump out at them and then chase them so that I can eat them. Woo-hoo!

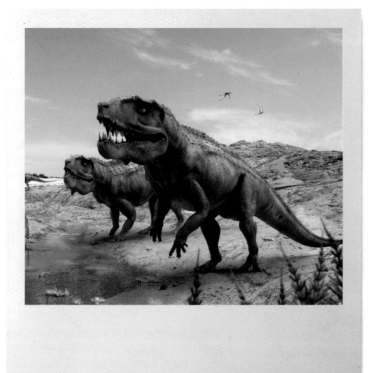

⭐ 30 LOVES

✒ #TEXASBABY! #LoneStarState. #DontMessWithTexas because now it's filled with #Humongous #Running crocodiles!

 DOUBLEDIPPER Yay Texas! #neighbors

 LONESTARLIZARD Didn't I just read you hurt yourself? #notscary #don'tmesswithyourself

35
photos

111
followers

264
following

Turkistan

Username: FEARLESSFLYER4EVER

Name: Longisquama (long-scales)

Period: Triassic (252–201 million years ago)

Size: 6 inches

Diet: Tinier insects

Hangouts: Turkistan

Bio: I'm all about living life on the edge. That's right! I'm a total daredevil. 😜 #noregrets #glideeveryday

⭐ **70 LOVES**
🚀 YOLO! #justjump

 CONCERNEDREPTILEPARENTS How DARE you! How dare you encourage our children to glide a little bit as they jump between branches! 😠

 FEARLESSFLYER4EVER I never said I was a #rolemodel. Now excuse me #whileikissthesky. #WHOOOOOOOOO 😎

52
photos

101
followers

223
following

South-
western
United
States

Username: DEZMAN1992

Name: Desmatosuchus

Period: Triassic (252–201 million years ago)

Size: 16 feet long

Diet: Plants on plants!

Hangouts: USA!

Bio: Sup! I'm Dez. Just a regular, reptile kind of guy with an upturned pig nose and a pair of back horns. I like movies, kickball, and plants. #nomnomnom

⭐ **16 LOVES**

〜 Another day means another chance to use my #backhorns. #DontLeaveHomeWithoutEm

 SUPADUPAFLY BTW, what do you actually use them for? Always been curious about that.

 DEZMAN1992 What DON'T I use them for is more like it. #everything

 SUPADUPAFLY What specifically, though?

 DEZMAN1992 Um. Like . . . to protect myself. #dontmesswithme

1 photos	
10 followers	
0 following	Argentina

Username: OLDMANHERRERASAURUS
Name: Herrerasaurus (Herrera's lizard)
Period: Triassic (231.4 million years ago)
Size: 4 feet tall, 13 feet long
Diet: Carnivore
Hangouts: Argentina
Bio: Greetings! Welcome to my official Internet web page. I am proud to be one of the first and oldest creatures called a "dinosaur."

★ 30 LOVES

🗘 #Greetings.

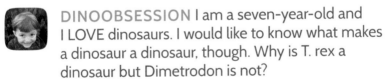

DINOOBSESSION I am a seven-year-old and I LOVE dinosaurs. I would like to know what makes a dinosaur a dinosaur, though. Why is T. rex a dinosaur but Dimetrodon is not?

OLDMANHERRERASAURUS For some reason, my message did not send. I pushed the button and instead of sending it, the message was erased. I hope this message goes through. Now I will type my message again. A dinosaur is a term that describes a large group of prehistoric reptiles with bodies that have many similarities.

70
photos

2,164
followers

407
following

Wales

Username: MILKYMORGAN

Name: Morganucodon

Period: Triassic to Jurassic (252–145 million years ago)

Size: 4 inches long, 1 ounce

Diet: Insects #slurp and other small animals

Hangouts: Wales, China

Bio: I'm one of the first mammals ever – I've got fur, I give birth to live young (no strange old eggs), and I feed them with milk!

Mouse Milk

★ **51 LOVES**

Okay, I'm sorta #smalltime right now. But I've got big dreams! My kids love my milk, and I think everyone else will, too! #MouseMilkEmpire. #MouseMilk4All. #StayTuned. #ComingSoon to a #TriassicSupermarket near you.

 #1_REPTILIA That's right! Dream big! Work hard! Make that money!

 SUPADUPAFLY Does your mouse milk empire sell Muscle Milk? #getfit

345
photos

2,716
followers

564
following

Germany

Username: NOODLENECKFISHING
Name: Tanystropheus (long-necked one)
Period: Triassic (252–201 million years ago)
Size: 20 feet long – 10 feet of which are my neck
Diet: Pescatarian #fisheater
Hangouts: Germany, Israel, Switzerland
Bio: I live for fishing! Let's just say I'm not a fan of #throwbackthursday – when I catch 'em, I eat 'em!

⭐ **541 LOVES**
✎ Gone fishin' #viewsfordays

 NOODLENECKFISHING sorta lonely out here, though. But who would ever want to go on a date with a guy whose neck is as long as his body and tail combined? 😢

 TANYSTRELLY_XO Hey, @noodleneckfishing, my neck is as long as my body and tail combined!

 NOODLENECKFISHINGFANATIC

125
photos

300
followers

175
following

Pangea

Username: PANGEAPARTAY

Name: Pangea (all the Earth)

Period: Paleozoic to Mesozoic (200–50 million years ago)

Size: The biggest, most incredible continent party of all time!

Hangouts: Everywhere

Bio: For hundreds of millions of years, all the continents were smashed up against one another. It absolutely rocked.

#werockas1

⭐ **24 LOVES**

〰️ #RememberWhen @NorthAmerica @SouthAmerica @Europe @Asia @Australia @Antarctica

 SOUTHAMERICA HAH! AWESOME pic. I had a blast chilling with all y'all.

 AFRICA Couldn't agree more! 😢 Sad we had to go our separate ways, but I'll cherish the memories of this party forever. It was just that sick!!

 NORTHAMERICA Exactly! So why wait another 200 million years to do it again? Let's just all instantly smash back into one another.

500
photos

427
followers

251
following

Great Britain

Username: COOLLILBRO

Name: Dimorphodon

Period: Jurassic (175–160 million years ago)

Size: 5 pounds, with a 4-foot wingspan

Diet: Fish and insects #greedy

Hangouts: Great Britain

Bio: I'm a lizard AND I'm an early pterosaur, which means "winged lizard." That's right, I can fly. Take THAT, @crocodiles. The only thing is I have just a touch of acrophobia. Oh, you don't know what that means? Um . . . well . . . it means I'm just the teeniest, tiniest bit afraid of heights.

⭐ 26 LOVES

 Nothin' to see up here. #TheGroundIsWhereIt'sAt

 COOLOLDERBRO Not this again! Dad said you're grounded if you keep telling people your secret! Dimorphodon up, bro!

201 photos

7,600 followers

521 following

Colorado

Username: POETASAURUS
Name: Stegosaurus ("Roof lizard")
Period: Jurassic (159–144 million years ago)
Size: 30 feet long
Diet: Plants
Hangouts: Colorado, Utah, Wyoming #westisthebest
Bio: Big dino with big plates. But don't let my size trick you – my mind is the biggest thing about me! Brains > Muscles ppl!!

⭐ **51 LOVES**

〽️ Yeah, yeah, yeah. Everybody always focuses on these #plates. Why not the #mind behind them? #smarts

 MEGASTEGA I thought our brains were the size of walnuts? 😬

 STEGZ Yeah, I always thought we had some of the smallest brains out of any dinosaurs.

 POETASAURUS Life lesson number one: you can't let anyone tell you what you can or can't do! Here's a poem I wrote about that very subject. It's called "Inspiration No. 1": Leaf. eat bark. swing tail. walk. eat. walk. walk around. eat leaf.

425 photos

707 followers

24 following

Western Europe

Username: BIRDSRDINOS
Name: Archaeopteryx
Period: Jurassic (150–148 million years ago)
Size: 1 foot long
Diet: Smaller creatures #LookOutBelow
Hangouts: Western Europe
Bio: All eyes on me, kids! I have some real important news to drop. That's right, you are never going to BELIEVE what I have to tell you. I look sorta like a bird, right? Well #spreadtheword: #BirdsAreDinosaurs and #DinosaursAreBirds! THIS. CHANGES. EVERYTHING.

200 LOVES

I believe I can fly. #FlyingDino #BirdsAreDinosToo

 AFRIENDLYPALEONTOLOGIST That's right, @BirdsRDinos! Birds are the last remaining line of dinosaurs! So dinosaurs still exist today!

 21STCENTURYPERSON Okay, okay. Very interesting. But when you say "dinosaurs still exist," people think, you know, ACTUAL dinosaurs still exist. Like @Official_Rex1. Or @b_rachs_rox. So how about we put all that "dinosaurs still exist" stuff on hold for a little? Until we got some "real" dinosaurs on the scene again?

374
photos

2,340
followers

567
following

Portugal

Username: ALTHEKING
Name: Allosaurus ("Different lizard." That's right – different!)
Period: Jurassic (155–150 million years ago)
Size: I'm about the size of a T. rex. Okay, I'm a little smaller. But smaller is better! That means I'm faster than a T. rex. Probably like a hundred times faster. A million times faster!
Diet: Meat! And, hey, who's to say it wasn't . . . I don't know, T. rex meat? I mean, 150 million years is a really long time ago. How can we say with any certainty that I didn't eat T. rexes?
Hangouts: Portugal
Bio: So crazy different. #unique

⭐ **10 LOVES**

✍️ #tbt to that time when I remembered I have #threefingers instead of boring old #two like @Official_Rex1. So #hilarious.

 ALTHEKING #crazy how much I can do with #threefingers that I couldn't do with two. 😬

 OFFICIAL_REX1 Only 10 loves @Altheking? #nobodylikesaliar #watchyourtail

 ALTHEKING Who's the real king? Sound off in the comments, fans! #AlvsOfficial_Rex1

893 photos

642 followers

439 following

Africa

Username: B_RACHS_ROX

Name: Brachiosaurus ("Arm lizard." Yeah. I mean, it's not the coolest name ever, but it was my grandfather's!)

Period: Jurassic to Cretaceous (156–145 million years ago)

Size: 50 feet tall. 5-foot-long head. So, yeah. I'm like your house. If it had six floors. And a 5-foot-long head. And was a dinosaur.

Diet: Delicious leaves at the tops of cycad trees. OMG, so good. Eat some now!

Hangouts: North America, Africa

Bio: Seriously. Go do it. I can tell that you aren't eating a cycad leaf right now. I'm not going to continue until there's a big cycad leaf in your mouth, being chewed.

★ 51 LOVES

⤴ Brontosaurus? Please. Turns out they never existed. I'm the #realdeal, though. One of the #tallestanimalsever. #WeatherUpHereIsNice #niceview

 THEREALBRONTSTER88 I . . . don't even know what to say . . . I bought this book because I was excited to learn about my ancestors . . . But you're saying I'm not even real? 😖

 B_RACHS_ROX Shoot, man, I'm sorry. I totally wasn't thinking. It's okay, though – your real name is Apatosaurus.

231
photos

652
followers

844
following

South
America

Username: SCENETEENOSAURUS

Name: Amargasaurus

Period: Cretaceous (130 million years ago)

Size: 30 feet long, 4,000 pounds, infinity miles of back spikes

Diet: Plants

Hangouts: South America

Bio: You can look, but you can't touch. See my two rows of spikes down by my neck and back? They're taller than your spikes. #spikelife. I #SufferForFashion

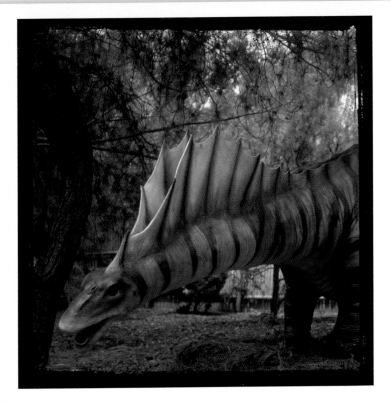

★ 73 LOVES

✐ Dinos may come and go, but my #PunkStyle will never die. #goth4life #sceneteen #emospikes #lookbutdoNOTtouch

 CAPTAIN_COOLIO Sweet sails, bro!

 HAIRTIPSFORSHARKS Hey! Get your own thing!

333 photos

629 followers

1,172 following

Egypt

Username: SPINOSAURUS1
Name: Spinosaurus
Period: Cretaceous (112–97 million years ago)
Size: 59 feet long, 22 tons, 6-foot-tall spines
Diet: Absolutely anything I want.
Hangouts: Egypt, Morocco
Bio: Yes, I'm deadly – as deadly as they come. But you know what? I keep it low-key. Why bring unwanted attention? I got a good thing going, and I don't wanna mess that up. #humble #blessed

★ **700 LOVES**

Lookin' good. #largestlandpredatorever. Yes, that means BIGGER than #ahem #coughcough #T_SomethingorOther. But you know what? I'm not jealous. I'm not in this for the fame.

 OFFICIAL_REX1 Well put, my friend. You do a great job of showing how not jealous you are. #sarcasm

256
photos

78
followers

2,921
following

Mongolia

Username: THEINFAMOUSVR
Name: Velociraptor
Period: Cretaceous (75–71 million years ago)
Size: About the size of a . . . let me just look in my "#historic" book about creatures from the future . . . Okay, about the size of a very large "chicken." I don't know what that is exactly, but I'm guessing it's a very large and scary monster.
Diet: All flesh, all the time.
Hangouts: Mongolia
Bio: Cretaceous's Most Wanted . . . perhaps you've heard of me? Even my name means "speedy thief." You may have heard of me, but you'll never see me. #badboy4lyfe

⭐ **81 LOVES**

Most people #KeepTheirDistance when they see me . . .
If only that were true of my little sister and her friends.
#SlumberPartyNight . . . #GetMeOuttaHere!

 VELOCISISTER Oh my gosh are you talking about us on here?! Just for that we're going to put some polish on your #RazorbladeClaws!!

 THEINFAMOUSVR No! Please! Leave me be!! 😳

 VELOCISISTER After we paint those claws . . . maybe your #PrettyFeathers will need some braiding!!! #MWAHAHAHA #EvilLaughEvilLaugh

121
photos

3,321
followers

629
following

Kansas

Username: IBITE

Name: Tylosaurus

Period: Late Cretaceous (88–80.5 million years ago)

Size: 40 feet long

Diet: Sharks, plesiosaurs, seabirds #whateverIfeellike

Hangouts: Kansas. When Kansas was underwater.

Bio: I'm a mosasaur: a giant, endlessly hungry lizard that lives in the sea. #DontCrossMe. And, yes, #iBite

⭐ **45 LOVES**

〽️ #Lunchstagram #RawPlesiosaurs #WithASideofSeabird

 MUCHOMOSASAUR Dude, you can't be posting pics like that . . . you could get in serious trouble.

 IBITE Yeah right. And how are they gonna pin these on me? If anyone asks, I'll just say it was photoshopped. #perfectcrime

 TIMEPOLICE @iBite, the citizens of the future have uncovered this fossil of you. A @Plesiosaur skull was found inside your stomach

 IBITE Uh-oh . . . @iBite2 did it!

661 photos

710 followers

892 following

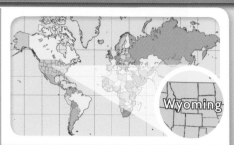

Wyoming

Username: KILLERSEAGIRAFFE22

Name: Elasmosaurus ("Thin-plated lizard." Please see below for more information on what to put on your plate to stay fit!)

Period: Cretaceous (145–66 million years ago)

Size: 46 feet long, 3 tons

Diet: Lean meat – but follow me for my secret, slimming tips!

Hangouts: Wyoming

Bio: I'm a plesiosaur – a long-necked swimming lizard. And I'd love to share some of my secret dieting tips with you! #Fit4Lyfe

16 LOVES

Flexy Friday. #EatPebbles #PebblesHelpWithDigestion #PebblesOnTheOceanFloor #EatThem #MiraclePebblesDiet

 KILLERSEAGIRAFFE22 Sorry for the spam, guys. I think I've been hacked by that "Eat Pebbles" virus that's been going around.

KILLERSEAGIRAFFE22 For the record, I do eat pebbles to aid in my digestion – that's why paleontologists find pebbles inside my fossils all the time.

1,213
photos

443
followers

646
following

Texas

Username: QUETZAKILLA
Name: Quetzalcoatlus
Period: Cretaceous (80–65 million years ago)
Size: 36-FOOT WINGSPAN. As tall as a giraffe!!
Diet: Most pterosaurs eat small fish. I eat large vertebrates – animals with spines.
Hangouts: Texas
Bio: I'm the biggest of all the pterosaurs. I was named after the Aztec god Quetzalcoatl. Because of my #UNBELIEVABLESIZE and #POWER and #FEROCITY. #FearMe

⭐ **1 LOVES**

〰️ Who else do you know that do it this big?
#SauropodSnacking

 SUSANQUETZ Honey, are you trying to be an
Internet tough guy again? You don't need to do
that, you know. We all love you for who you are –
#sweet #sensitive #silly

 QUETZAKILLA MOM!!!! Get OUT of here! 🙄

 SUSANQUETZ Okay, okay! Sorry, sweetie. Lots of
love to the biggest little guy I know! –Mommy
P.S. Lots of kisses too! 😘

846
photos

901
followers

732
following

Mongolia

Username: NOTHINGBUTNAILS
Name: Therizinosaurus (scythe lizard)
Period: Cretaceous (75–70 million years ago)
Size: Almost as big as a T. rex. But . . .
Diet: . . . I just eat plants even though I have 2-foot-long, unbelievably sharp claws.
Hangouts: Mongolia, Kazakhstan, Russia
Bio: If I could wish for anything, it would be for world peace. Can't we all just get along, @Official_Rex1? Nice guys finish first.
#bekind #grateful

⭐ **22 LOVES**

✏️ Be kind to one another. #worldpeace #DinosThatWorkTogetherStayTogether #equality #QOTD

 OFFICIAL_REX1 All dinos are not created equal. #sorrynotsorry

230 photos

461 followers

524 following

North America

Username: DUCKFACEZ
Name: Parasaurolophus
Period: Cretaceous (76.5–73 million years ago)
Size: 40 feet tall with a 6-foot-tall crest
Diet: Devoted vegetarian. #meatkills
Hangouts: North America
Bio: #WeirdfactWednesday: behind my #duckbill, I've got thousands of teeth. Thousands! haha! How crazy is that?! #originalduckface

★ 300 LOVES

No – the #DuckFace is NOT just a pose for pictures! We use these babies (and the cool things on our heads) to communicate in the deep forests. And also because it's NEVER wrong to #DuckFace. #CantStopWontStop

 HAIRTIPSFORSHARKS Hi there! Ignore my user name! Everyone's hair needs a little love! Check out my page to found out how to handle that do!

561 photos

251 followers

263 following

South Dakota

Username: NEATOTURTLITO

Name: Archelon

Period: Cretaceous (100–66 million years ago)

Size: About the length of 12 foot-long rulers laid end to end, and roughly the width of 16 foot-long rulers also laid end to end. I wonder if there's an easier way to say that . . .

Diet: Squid squid squid. #CanIHaveThisFried? #calamari

Hangouts: South Dakota, Wyoming

Bio: Biggest turtle of all time. #OhYeahBaby!

⭐ **58 LOVES**

✏️ Fell asleep on the ocean floor and then #IWokeUpLikeThis. Just in time for #FossilFriday! 😎

 NOTHINGBUTNAILS You look so #peaceful

299
photos

443
followers

2,008
following

South Dakota

Username: BONEDOMESMASHER
Name: Pachycephalosaurus
Period: Cretaceous (72–66 million years ago)
Size: 16 feet long, 950 pounds. Big head dome, good for smash.
Diet: Smash plants with mini bone domes inside mouth. Smash smash smash. Smash smash smash. Swallow swallow swallow.
Hangouts: Montana, Wyoming, South Dakota
Bio: Have bone dome on head. Fun to smash. Lives in herds. Likes to smash head on friends.

⭐ **300 LOVES**

📷 Welcome to the dome zone. #smashbrothers

 KILLERSEAGIRAFFE22 Hey there! I saw that you're in the Cretaceous period. I just moved in here! What do you guys do for fun?

 BONEDOMESMASHER #domesmash 😬

 KILLERSEAGIRAFFE22 I'm sorry?

 BONEDOMESMASHER #smashdome

245
photos

3,972
followers

6,158
following

New
Mexico

Username: PENTACERA45
Name: Pentaceratops (five-horned face)
Period: Cretaceous (75–73 million years ago)
Size: 20 feet, 8 tons
Diet: All the plants I can get my beak on
Hangouts: New Mexico
Bio: I'm a father first, husband second, and ceratopsian
third. Family is the most important thing to me in the world.
#AllYouNeedIsLove

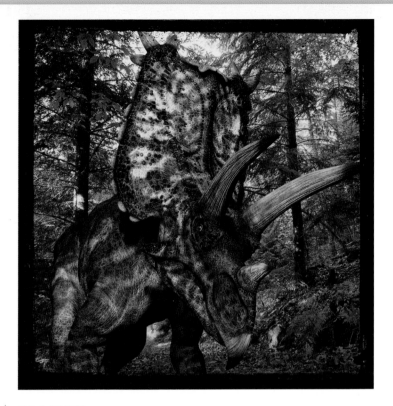

⭐ **50 LOVES**

✏️ Home-improvement day! Working on a brand-new nest for @MrsPentacera and our soon-to-be-laid #ClutchOfEggs. #StepOne: Soften some of the ground up with my beak.

 PENTACERA45 Hmm . . . those horns are stuck in there #realgood. #shoot.

 @MRSPENTACERA That's okay, pookieceras, it's the thought that counts. <3 #StillLoveYou #4lyfe #LittleHelp, people? #LittleHelp.

 PENTACERA45 Oh, why do all my #homeimprovementprojects have to end this way?

506 photos

12,600 followers

7,916 following

Gobi Desert

Username: FLEETFOOT23

Name: Gallimimus (rooster mimic)

Period: Cretaceous (70 million years ago)

Size: 20 feet long, 6 feet off the ground (best way to practice a proper running stance)

Diet: Herbivorous. Because achieving your best time isn't just about working out – it's about eating right, too. #eatclean

Hangouts: Gobi Desert

Bio: I guess you could say I'm a speed freak. Translation? Running is my passion. I pursue excellence every day. I run this desert. #ItWasAllABlur

★ 801 LOVES

Hit #30to40mph today while training. Feeling unbelievable. #crushingit #fartherfasterstronger #instafit #workouttime #catchup

 PROTOCERATOPSMOMMY Is it normal to feel bad about myself whenever I look at your feed? 😢

 FLEETFOOT23 Yes.

222
photos

0
followers

1.3M
following

United States

Username: OFFICIAL_REX1

Name: Tyrannosaurus rex. (In the process of changing my name to Tyrockstarosaurus Rexington. #rebranding)

Period: Cretaceous (68–65 million years ago. Kickin' back for the last 66 million years – and still the most famous dino!)

Size: Huge. Gigantic. Colossal.

Diet: I kill stuff and eat it. I find dead stuff and eat it. #special.

Hangouts: USA, Canada, Mongolia, TV, Internet, Movies

Bio: Yo, @triceratops, I'm really happy for you, and I'll let you finish, but I had the best photo of all time! Even my name means "king!" Everybody's scared of me cuz I'm the biggest carnivore around. Just one thing, why won't anyone follow me?!

★ 0 LOVES

～! Anybody out there? I'll find you. #selfiesunday

 PLESIOSAURUS @official_rex1, not me! T. rexes can't swim LOL!!

 OFFICIAL_REX1 Guess you've never seen my #dinopaddle. Here I come @Plesiosaurus!

 PLESIOSAURUS AHHHHHHHHHHHHHHHHHHHHHHHHHHHHH!!!!

222 photos

0 followers

1.3M following

Canada

Username: SLOWANDSTEADY
Name: Euoplocephalus ("Well-armored head." Could it be any lamer? Why can't I have some cool name?)
Period: Cretaceous (76.5–75.6 million years ago)
Size: 20 feet long, two tons
Diet: Roots and tubers
Hangouts: Canada
Bio: I'm a member of the Ankylosaurus family. We're all covered in bony plates and have these tails that are like clubs. Trust me, it sounds cooler than it is. It's only there because we're too big and slow to run away from our predators.

⭐ **58 LOVES**

〰 #selfie #ew #bulkcentral #lumpytail #imsogigantic #awkward

 NOTHINGBUTNAILS NOOOOO. You are GORGEOUS!!!!

 SLOWANDSTEADY haha ur way too nice . . . no need to lie to me, though, know i'm #spiky and #ugly . . . and these bone plates are like #gross. 😦

 NOTHINGBUTNAILS OMG! QUIT IT! You're SOOOO gorgeous #loveyourself

| 1 |
| photos |
| 0 |
| followers |
| 1M |
| following |

World-wide

Username: CRETACEOUSDEATHSTORM
Name: The Cretaceous–Paleogene Extinction, aka the K–Pg extinction
Period: 66 million years ago
Diet: 80% of all species
Hangouts: Worldwide
Bio: Let's just cut to the chase here: I'm kind of the party pooper. The dinosaurs had their time. On to the next one! #yolo

★ **92 LOVES**

〲 #massivecomet with the energy of #onebillionnukes. #dustcloud so large that it covers the sun for a year. #ByeByeDinos

 OFFICIAL_REX1 Hey, hey, hey! Just heard that there might be some sort of cataclysmic #extinctionevent! Wow, I hate to be #thatguy, but I was wondering – any chance I could get a little, you know, #startreatment? 😎

 CRETACEOUSDEATHSTORM Well . . . why not? Come stand over here . . . yep, right in that spot, very nice . . . Stay nice and still . . . and now look up at that "star" in the sky. Enjoy!

272 photos

6,417 followers

1,023 following

Username: THEREALBIGBIRD

Name: Phorusrhacid ("Scar-bearer." But all my friends just call me #terrorbird)

Period: Paleocene to Pleistocene (4.9–1.8 million years ago)

Size: 10 feet tall

Diet: Meeeaaat

Hangouts: South America, North America

Bio: Big Bird? Great guy, great guy. But let's just say I'm gonna be the #NextBigThing. I can kung fu kick. Did that yellow guy ever do that?

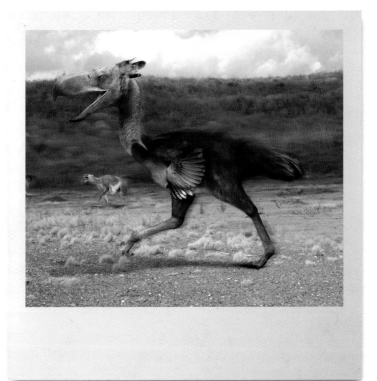

★ 51 LOVES

.! #ReadyForMyCloseup! I'm just like your favorite fluffy yellow guy. But I'm #10FeetTall. And #DeadlyFast. With a beak that'll cut you in half.

 THEREALBIGBIRD In other words, how can you NOT make me the star of a show for three- and four-year-olds?

101
photos

631
followers

812
following

Tropics of South America

Username: CUDDLYCONSTRICTOR

Name: Titanoboa ("Titanic boa." Like, maybe a larger version of my cousin the boa constrictor, I guess. But what if that "boa" is actually there to make you think of bows? Like pretty bows wrapped around beautiful presents I got for you!)

Period: Paleocene (60–58 million years ago)

Size: 42 feet long, 2,500 pounds – of friendship 😀

Diet: Weird question! LOL! Come on, who cares?! It's not like what I eat is weird or scary or anything. Let's just move on.

Hangouts: Tropics of South America

Bio: Ha-ha, come on, enough about me already! Let's talk about you. You're in need of a hug, aren't you?

★ 201 LOVES

✎ #JustOneOfThoseDays . . . You know, the kind where you're #InNeedOfAHug? You're my friend, right? Waddya say? Hug it out?

 CUDDLYCONSTRICTOR LOL, no responses . . . #Really? I promise this isn't a way to trick you into being squeezed to death and eaten by me.

 CUDDLYCONSTRICTOR Srsly, nobody? #WasItSomethingISaid?

22 photos
764 followers
981 following

Utah

Username: FANTASTICFURREDFLYER
Name: Icaronycteris (Icarus night flyer)
Period: Eocene (55–34 million years ago)
Size: Roughly the size of a small, flying rodent.
Diet: Insects. Like, flying ones. In the air. And I'm in the air, too. Flying. But I'm not a bird! I'm a mammal! Can you believe that? I'm basically like . . . a flying dog!
Hangouts: Colorado, Wyoming, Utah
Bio: Totally unbelievable beast. I might as well be out of some science fiction story. I mean – a flying mammal. You're a mammal, right?! So actually, I'm like a flying YOU.

⭐ 7 LOVES

~ #faroutfriday #mammal . . . but #IBelieveICanFly. The question is, CAN YOU believe it?

 AFRIENDLYPALEONTOLOGIST Sure we can! You are an ancestor of modern-day bats – flying mammals that everyone knows! In fact, you look a ton like those modern bats.

 FANTASTICFURREDFLYER But can these amazing "modern-day bats" of yours find their food through echolocation?

 AFRIENDLYPALEONTOLOGIST That is a great question! Yes, they can.

101 photos
299 followers
3,171 following

Plains of Mongolia

Username: CARNIVORIAGLORIA

Name: Andrewsarchus

Period: Eocene (45–36 million years ago)

Size: 13 feet long, 2,000 pounds, appetite for days

Diet: Meat, meat, meat. And did I happen to mention: meat? Oh, yes. Yes, I did. Well, why not do it one more time, then? MEAT!

Hangouts: Mongolian Plains

Bio: I'm Gloria. But you can just call me The Giant, Long-Headed Dog-Looking Thing That's About To Eat You.

⭐ **51 LOVES**

~ #meatlessmondays? Yeah, right. How about . . .
#MeatMOREMondays! Or #EatMoreMeatMoreMondays
. . . um . . . #more. #meat. #eatsome. Fine, so I'm
not the greatest hashtag creator ever. But I AM the
#TopCarnivore of the Eocene! #illeat2that

 THEREALBIGBIRD LOL! Right on
@Carnivoriagloria I love meat, too. Wanna meat,
I mean meet for dinner? #it'snotadate

12
photos

465
followers

912
following

Plains of Asia

Username: SLAMMAJAMMAMAMMA

Name: Indricotherium

Period: Oligocene to Miocene (30 to 16.6 million years ago)

Size: 40 feet long, 40,000 pounds

Diet: To stay on top, I eat #AnUnbelievableAmountOfLeaves Everyday.

Hangouts: The plains of Asia

Bio: I'm the biggest land mammal that ever lived – in fact, nearly as big as some of the guys in the Brachiosaurus family. Perfect for #BasketballDomination!

⭐ **51 LOVES**

#SheShootsSheScores! #SlammaJammaExtraordinaire! #TheBestThereIs! Now if only anyone else in prehistory played basketball. #Sigh. Maybe I'll #TakeMyTalents to the #Future.

 SUPADUPAFLY You're ripped @slammajammamamma! #fitness

 NOODLENECKFISHING I'm tall. I can ball. Pick me!

10
photos

201
followers

760
following

The Plains of Eurasia

Username: MOROPUSOBSESSED

Name: Moropus

Period: Miocene (23–13.6 million years ago)

Size: 10 feet tall. One ton. Style for days.

Diet: I eat plants. Just like @Moropus3!!!! We have so much in common! <3 <3

Hangouts: The plains (and runways) of Eurasia

Bio: You guys! How cute is @Moropus3? He is just so dreamy. That's why I started this page with all of his best photos. #marryme #junewedding

MOROPUS

★ 67 LOVES

✎ Man crush Monday. How adorable is @Moropus3 just walking on his knuckles? Horse + Gorilla = moropus. 🙊💐 #MCM

 MOROPUS3 Aw Shucks.

 MOROPUSOBSESSED OMG!! You spoke to me! #dying

301 photos
291 followers
146 following

Africa

Username: SHOVELEPHANT
Name: Platybelodon
Period: Miocene (15–4 million years ago)
Size: 9 feet tall with a big ol' flop-o mouth
Diet: Sweet, sweet bark, which my mouth is designed to scrape off. Man, I'm getting hungry just THINKING about that bark!
Hangouts: Africa, Europe, Asia, North America
Bio: One of many different species of prehistoric elephant – but I'm the ONLY one who's got an insane #ShovelMouth. #winning

⭐ **67 LOVES**

✐ How are YOU celebrating #NationalShovelMouthDay?? #LIKE this picture if you're duct-taping a shovel onto your face. #COMMENT if you're forcing your parents to get you some braces that stretch your mouth to the ground and give you two #BuckTeeth.

 DUCKFACEZ That's a pretty good face, but not as pretty as #duckface!

200
photos

121
followers

646
following

Peru

Username: SURFERSLOTHMAXIMUS
Name: Thalassocnus (sea sloth)
Period: Miocene to Pliocene (10–2 million years ago)
Size: 6 feet long, 500 pounds, chill for days
Diet: Seagrass, seaweed, seaburgers (a super-chill species of #LivingHamburger during the Miocene that all the chilliest water-dwelling prehistoric creatures ate)
Hangouts: Peru, Chile, Coastin' Down South America
Bio: What's cooler than being a super-chill sloth? #nothing! How about a super-chill giant prehistoric swimming sloth? #evenMOREnothing!!

⭐ **43 LOVES**

〽️ Catchin some waves #chillin #seaside #SlothStyle

 CHILLPREHISTORICJELLYFISH Sup, g! You wanna come over to 500 million years ago and chill?

 SURFERSLOTHMAXIMUS 😎 #ButOfCourse.

 SURFERSLOTHMAXIMUS (To all my human buddies reading this, I forgot to mention that in addition to living seaburgers, another thing that went extinct was living, swimming time machines. They're so fun. Don't you guys agree?)

760
photos

491
followers

326
following

South America

Username: TINYTRUNKSRCOOL

Name: Macrauchenia (long llama)

Period: Miocene to Pleistocene (7 million–10 thousand years ago)

Size: 10 feet long with a nose that's sorta like a dangling Slinky

Diet: Do you know how many plants I can eat with this thing?

Hangouts: South America

Bio: Mom says my trunk gives me character. Shout-out to all my buddies in the herd! #socialcreature

★ 67 LOVES

✒ What a great day with my BFF! #7MillionHappyYears #Year1

 SHOVELEPHANT What kind of trunk is that? #where'stheshovel

O
photos

O
followers

O
following

North America

Username: UNDERGROUNDCRAFTS

Name: Ceratogaulus

Period: Miocene (10–5 million years ago)

Size: 1 gophersworth + 1 hornsworth

Diet: Roots, insects, and any number of delicious appetizers you can make yourself!

Hangouts: Woodlands of North America

Bio: Okay, so my name means "horned gopher" and, yes, I spend a lot of time digging. But that's not my only hobby! I love to #CRAFT, and I thought I'd share my passions with the world!

⭐ 67 LOVES

〽️ #CraftOfTheDay: a hole to live inside! First #dig in the dirt with your #longclaws to make a burrow. Now, use your #horns as a #partyhat to celebrate your new home! #cozy #DIY #artsandcrafts

 AFRIENDLYPALEONTOLOGIST Beautiful pictures! Now, what if you don't have horns or claws? Can you still do #artsandcrafts?

 UNDERGROUNDCRAFTS No.

52
photos

1,232
followers

3,764
following

South America

Username: MRSABERTOYOU
Name: Smilodon
Period: Pleistocene (2.6 million years ago–11,700 years ago)
Size: About the size of a lion, but heavier
Diet: Sloths, horses, and, camels, oh my!
Hangouts: South America
Bio: Everyone says I'm a tiger, but really I'm a cat. Don't get it twisted. You don't want to mess with this pet! Have you seen these teeth? #catnottiger

⭐ **44 LOVES**

〜 You're gonna hear me roar! #20inchteeth

 BIGWOOLLYSTYLES You call those things big? My tusks are 17 feet long.

 MRSABERTOYOU That's the only thing big about you, @BigWoollyStyles. You're only as big as an African elephant. haha! #notamammoth

701
photos

2,220
followers

3,120
following

Europe

Username: BIGWOOLLYSTYLES
Name: Woolly Mammoth
Period: Pliocene (5 million–4,500 years ago)
Size: Slightly smaller than modern elephants
Diet: Birch trees, grasses, sedges
Hangouts: Europe, Africa, Asia, North America
Bio: Hi, lady woollys. I'm single and lookin'! I may have put on a little #winterweight but I'm nowhere near MAMMOTH like some people say. I'm a lean, mean, adorable machine! Let's take a walk on the ice!

⭐ **67 LOVES**

 Class picture ready. #goodhairday #pearlywhitetusks

 SHOVELEPHANT Lookin' good! Love those tusks. You're totally going to win best smile in the yearbook. #winning

121 photos

300 followers

237 following

North America

Username: SPORTYBEAV

Name: Castoroides

Period: Pliocene to Pleistocene (3 million–10,000 years ago)

Size: As long as the tallest human who ever lived. Not bad for a beaver, I must say.

Diet: Reeds and grasses – breakfast of champions!

Hangouts: North America

Bio: I live for competition!

1ST PLACE
Tree Racing Competition

TEAM RODENT!

★ 51 LOVES

Go #TeamRodent! Come by the GIANT NORTH AMERICAN PREHISTORIC MAMMALS CHAMPIONSHIP and watch me compete. I'll be in two events: my specialty, the Tree Eating Competition, and some other event called the Giant Beaver Being Eaten By Saber Tooth Cat Competition. I'm not sure why the second one is called that, and honestly, I don't have time to do any research about it at all. Well, I'm off to the games! #TeamRodentFTW!

 MILKYMORGON Mammals unite! You should try some #mousemilk for a balanced breakfast. #goodluck

2,461 photos

10,300 followers

5,172 following

Southern Russia

Username: DAPARTYBEAST

Name: Elasmotherium (thin-plate monster)

Period: Pleistocene (2.5 million–50,000 years ago)

Size: 26 feet long – with a 6.5 foot horn! YEAH! WE DO IT BIG AROUND HERE!

Diet: Oh, man – all the tastiest grass, 24/7. Having a sick giant horn like this – it's not just fun and games all the time. Like, it's heavy and stuff! And people always want to touch it. So, yeah, I reward myself with the most delicious grass.

Hangouts: Southern Russia, Siberia

Bio: I'm an ancient rhinoceros – but just because I'm old doesn't mean I can't throw down! You think different? Tell it to the horn!

⭐ 26 LOVES

📣 Hitting the town tonight rocking the #FreshestHorn that's #tallerthanyourdad. #partyallthetime

 BIGWOOLLYSTYLES Dunno, dude . . . you might wanna chill on that. Like now that humans are on the scene we might just wanna keep a low profile . . . they seem #madextincty.

 DAPARTYBEAST Pssh. Have fun with that. I'm gonna #keepthepartygoing. 😎

272
photos

891
followers

342
following

South America

Username: SAFETYFIRST

Name: Glyptodon

Period: Pliocene to Pleistocene (2.5 million years ago to 10,000 years ago)

Size: 10 feet long, 2,000 pounds, one big shell

Diet: Grass, good old nonthreatening, nondangerous grass

Hangouts: South America

Bio: Even though it might not be "#cool" or "#hip" or "a #GoodWayToMakeFriends," be like me and always wear a helmet! A full-body helmet covering almost every inch of your flesh. At all times.

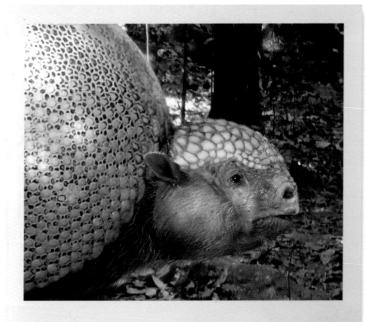

⭐ **112 LOVES**

〜 Remember: it's dangerous out there! #Safetyfirst!!

 TANKSTERINO Awesome helmet man! That looks newer than mine. #Jealous

217 photos

445 followers

631 following

Australia

Username: LIZARDFROMOZ
Name: Megalania (giant roamer)
Period: Pleistocene to Modern (2 million–30,000 years ago)
Size: 25 feet long, 4,000 pounds
Diet: Anything! Not a #PickyEater. I mean, as long as it's a #GiantPrehistoricMarsupial, I'm happy.
Hangouts: Australia #LandDownUnder, baby!
Bio: G'day, mates! I'm an unbelievably giant meat-eating lizard from the #LandDownUnder!

⭐ **71 LOVES**

〜 Time for a little #Q&A! What do YOU want to know about living in the past as a giant prehistoric creature? #AskAway #LizardTipTuesday

 SOCCER4LIFE2002 You're in Australia, right?

 LIZARDFROMOZ Yep! I was around when you guys first got here, in fact!

 SOCCER4LIFE2002 Cool, cool. So do the toilets really run backward down there?

100 photos

6.2B followers

20M following

Northern India

Username: GIANTAPEQUESTIONS

Name: Gigantopithecus (Giant Ape)

Period: Miocene to Pleistocene (9 million–100,000 years ago)

Size: About 2 gorillas stacked together

Diet: Bamboo

Hangouts: Northern India, China

Bio: Not all #GiantApes are #KingKongs. #LoverNotAFighter #smarterthanyouraveragegorilla

★ 150 LOVES

Here I am. In my #naturalhabitat. It's #peaceful and #serene in these mountain ranges.

 HUMAN That seems like a nice place to live . . .

PALEOZOIC ERA

MILLIONS OF YEARS AGO

550

500

450

400

350

300

250

Cambrian Period
542–488 mya
Age of Marine Invertebrates
First organisms with shells or external skeletons appear. Oceans full of creatures including brachiopods, which resemble modern-day clams, and arthropods, which are ancestors of insects, spiders, and crustaceans. Primitive corals and fish develop.

Silurian Period
443–416 mya
Rise of Land Animals
Jawed fish, evolved corals, and sponges appear. First true land plants emerge. Millipedes, some six feet long, and early spiders and mites creep onto land.

Carboniferous Period
360–300 mya
Rise of Reptiles
Development of amniotic egg allows early reptiles to inhabit and reproduce on land. Plentiful vegetation leads to an increase in oxygen in the atmosphere. Six-foot-long centipedes and three-foot-long cockroaches roam the growing forests. Amphibians also grow in size. Winged insects take to the air.

PALEOZOIC ERA

550

500

Ordovian Period
488–443 mya
Rise of the Fish
Sea life triples and includes trilobites, who are the earliest-known animal to have vision, nautiloids that look like squids, and eels with backbones, called conodonts. Horseshoe crabs crawl onto land. Primitive corals and fish develop.

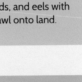

450

400

Devonian Period
416–360 mya
Age of Fishes / Rise of Amphibians
Ancestors to sharks and rays called cartilaginous fish thrive in oceans. Amphibious creatures called tetrapods, develop from bony fishes, ancestors of all four-limbed land vertebrates. Primitive insects arrive on the scene. First plants with roots emerge.

350

300

Permian Period
300–250 mya
Reptilian Diversification
Early reptiles–therapsids–split to become carnivores or herbivores, some sporting "sails" on their backs to collect heat from the sun. Seas are full with scaled bony fishes. Roaches, termites, and bees develop.

250

MILLIONS OF YEARS AGO

PALEOZOIC ERA

MILLIONS OF YEARS AGO

250

MESOZOIC ERA

200

150

100

CENOZOIC ERA
Tertiary Period

50

The Permian Extinction
250 mya
More than 90 percent of all marine species and 70 percent of land animals are wiped out. One theory is that debris from massive volcanic eruptions blocks out the sun, causing drops in temperature and the inability of plants to reproduce.

Triassic Period
250–200 mya
Age of Reptiles
Reptiles that survive the Permian Extinction develop into the first dinosaurs. Some rise off four feet into upright postures; others become the first flying reptiles, called pterosaurs. The earliest true mammal, a shrewlike creature that gives birth to live young, appears. Amphibious creatures flourish, including primitive crocodiles.

Cretaceous Period
144–65 mya
Dinosaur Shifts
New species of dinosaurs appear as older ones settle in specific northern or southern climatological areas, some forming herds. Frogs, turtles, and snakes occupy the coastlines. Sharks resemble those of modern day. Primitive birds quickly acquire distinctive characteristics. Flowering plants, including grasses and hardwood trees, appear. Butterflies, moths, beetles, and ants thrive.

PALEOZOIC ERA

250

MESOZOIC ERA

Pangea
270–200 mya
Continental Shifts
Pangea, a mash-up of all our present-day continents created by movement of Earth's tectonic plates, begins to split up. The breakup of Pangea over the course of time leads both to extinctions and developments of plant and animal species.

200

150

MILLIONS OF YEARS AGO

Jurassic Period
200–144 mya
Dinosaur Domination
Dinosaurs become more numerous and more diversified. Oceans swarm with huge plesiosaurs, giant crocodiles and sharks, and tiny plankton. Earliest known bird, *Archaeopteryx*, flies alongside pterosaurs. Small early mammals the size of rats live among abundant plant life.

100

The Cretaceous-Paleogene Extinction
65 mya
Dinosaurs and most land animals under 55 pounds become extinct between the Cretaceous and Paleogene Periods. Scientists still debate the cause, but agree that debris blocks out sunlight and destroys plant life on land and in the seas. One theory claims this was once again caused by massive volcanic activity. Another theory suggests that a giant asteroid or comet hit Earth.

CENOZOIC ERA
Tertiary Period

50

CENOZOIC ERA
Tertiary Period

50

40

MILLIONS OF YEARS AGO

30

20

CENOZOIC ERA
Quaternary Period

10

Eocene Epoch
56–34 mya
Odd-Toes and Even-Toes
Two new groups of hoofed animals called ungulates appear: odd-toed like horses, rhinoceroses, and tapirs, and even-toed like deer, cattle, and sheep. First appearances of modern whales, porpoises, and dolphins, and primitive manatees and dugongs. Primitive elephants and bats develop.

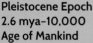

Miocene Epoch
23–5 mya
Primate Explosion
Higher primates, including apes and gibbons, are recorded, and distinguished from the lower primates like lemurs, lorises, and tarsiers. Land-dwelling mammals are essentially modern. Bears, hyenas, and saber-tooth cats, and primitive giraffes, seals, and walruses appear. Archaic elephants spread from Africa to Asia. Birds fly over all continents.

Pleistocene Epoch
2.6 mya–10,000
Age of Mankind
Long-horned bison, giant ground sloths, horses, camels, mammoths, and other large land mammals flourish in North America, all of which go extinct by the end of the epoch. The human species appears.

Paleocene Epoch
65–56 mya
Age of Mammals
Continents are almost in their present position. The first whales appear, the descendants of land mammals. Woodlands and grasslands grow, as do herds of grazing hoofed mammals. "Archaic" forms of dogs, cats, rats, and rabbits appear. In tropical and subtropical areas, early primates develop rotating shoulder joints, three-dimensional vision, and hands that can grasp.

50

40

Oligocene Epoch
34–23 mya
Short but Sweet
Mammals continue to diversify and specialize. First recorded appearance of camels and pigs. Earliest apelike animals and New World monkeys appear.

30

MILLIONS OF YEARS AGO

20

Pliocene Epoch
5.3–2.6 mya
Getting Back Together
The North and South American continents are reconnected. Animals known only in South America–ground sloths–armadillos, opossums, and porcupines now appear in North America. Woolly mammoths and mastodons roam through all landmasses. The first hominids–*australopithecines*–appear. The most recent glaciation (ice age) begins.

CENOZOIC ERA
Quaternary Period

10